Alexander Peskanov's

THE RUSSIAN TECHNICAL REGIMEN

FOR THE PIANO

(Series of Six Books)

Exercise Volume II

BROKEN CHORDS

Technical Editor - Lynn Radcliffe

W.M. Co. 11614E

W.M. Co. 11614E

To
My Beloved Teachers in Russia,
ROSALIA MOLODIETZKAYA and her son, EMIL

IN GRATEFUL REMEMBRANCE

Cover Illustration by LYNN RADCLIFFE

W.M. Co. 11614E

Concert pianist and composer, appeared as soloist with London Philharmonic, English Chamber Orchestra, National Symphony and orchestras of Baltimore, St. Louis, Houston, Utah and others. Concertized in 48 states and 20 countries on four continents. Recipient of ASCAP awards for music and theater compositions. Graduated from Stoliarsky School of Music, Odessa, Ukraine, and received Masters Degree from Julliard School of Music, New York. Married to Lu Ann, concert flutist and teacher; has two children.

ALEXANDER PESKANOV

Author

Music/piano enthusiast, retired from career in the aerospace industry. Was record reviewer for American Record Guide Magazine, artist. Graduated with BS degree from Syracuse University, 1942. Married to Jean; has two children.

LYNN E. RADCLIFFE

Technical Editor

* * * * * * * * * * * * * * * * * * * *

Lynn Radcliffe and I started our relationship with a fair exchange: he told me about traveling in space and I told him about playing double thirds and broken chords. Lynn was one of the first people to whom I introduced elements of the Russian Technical Regimen for piano. Each of us added a new dimension to the other's life, and we found that we shared one significant quality in our characters: endless curiosity in the pursuit of knowledge. Discovering that this regimen is just as effective for a person of sixty-eight and beyond as it is for a child of ten has inspired us to write this series of books for students of all ages.

Alexander Peskanov

FOREWORD

This exercise volume is part of a series of books entitled *The Russian Technical Regimen for the Piano*. It consists of the INTRODUCTION AND GUIDE to the regimen and five exercise volumes. The Russian Technical Regimen encompasses all the technical requirements which have been in use in Russian and Soviet music schools and conservatories for more than a century.

This exercise volume presents eleven broken chords in the Russian harmonic pattern, starting from all twelve notes. The eleven broken chords starting from C should serve as an example for the transpositions of the same harmonic pattern of eleven chords starting from other notes. In other words, all the chords, starting from any note, should eventually be practiced both hands, four octaves up and down in parallel motion. This eleven-chord pattern, as well as detailed instructions on how to perform broken chords, is explained in the INTRODUCTION AND GUIDE to *The Russian Technical Regimen for the Piano,* Part Three, Chapter XIII. It should be noted that, as in the example starting from C, the first six broken chords are presented in "threes" and also in "fours." These two rhythms should be exercised in practicing the first six broken chords from all other notes. While accenting in "threes", the downbeat comes on a different finger each time. This does not occur when accenting in "fours." The last five chords are accented in "fours" where there is a different finger on each downbeat. These accents provide equal opportunity to develop all five fingers. The broken-chord exercises are vitally important in developing well-coordinated wrists and fingers. They also allow the hands to achieve the maximum flexibility and mobility at the keyboard.

In all phases of *The Russian Technical Regimen for the Piano* accents must always be the foundation for the rhythm and points of relaxation. The benefits of the Regimen can accrue only if it is practiced in the proper manner with full realization of the Guide Book instructions.

Alexander Peskanov

Supplementary materials and additional teaching aids include:

Introduction and Guide ("Guide Book")

Exercise Volume I, Scales in Single Notes

Exercise Volume II, Broken Chords

Exercise Volume III, Russian Broken Chords

Exercise Volume IV, Arpeggios and Block Chords

Exercise Volume V, Scales in Double Notes: Thirds, Sixths, Octaves

Instructional Videos, "In Search of Sound"
        Produced by Classical Video Concepts, Inc.

Piano Olympics Kit, Manual and Demonstration Video
        Produced by CVC, Inc.

Piano Video Exchange, Presented by the Baldwin Piano
        and Organ Co. and CVC, Inc.

Six Broken Chords Starting from C*

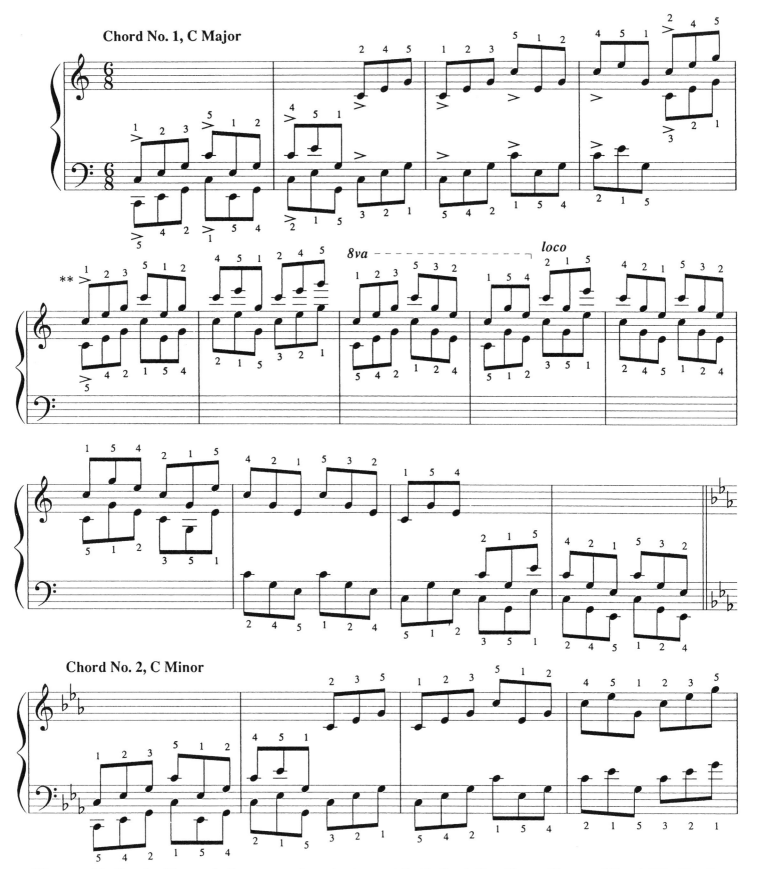

*Presented in Russian Harmonic Pattern; see *Introduction and Guide Book,* Part Three, Chapters VI and VII. The first six chords of eleven here are in 6/8 meter (3 notes on one wrist motion with accent on downbeat of each group of three).
**Accent every downbeat in each group of three notes.

Chord No. 3, A♭ Major 6

*Use 4 (L.H.) rather than 3 because 4 is not obstructed as in chord No.1 from E flat (page 22). There is identical fingering in L.H. (5-4-2-1) in A flat major and D flat major chords, (root position), and a 5-3-2-1 pattern in E flat major and B flat major chords, (root position).

Chord No. 4, A Minor 6

Chord No. 5, F Major $\frac{6}{4}$

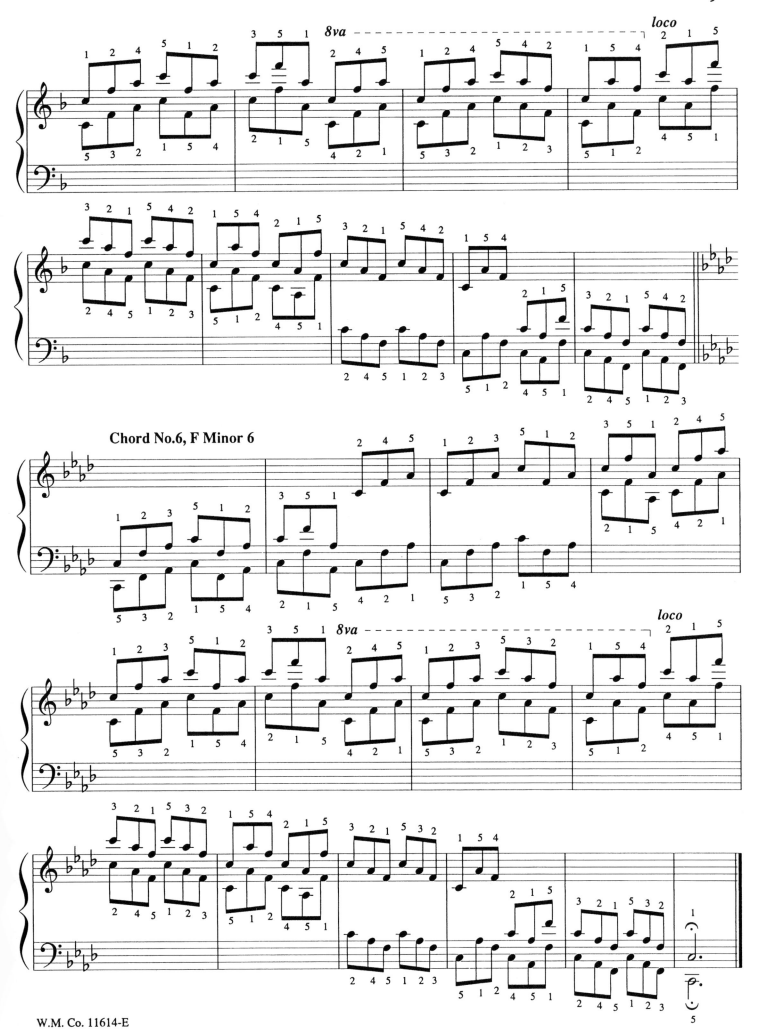

Chord No.6, F Minor 6

Eleven Broken Chords Starting from C*

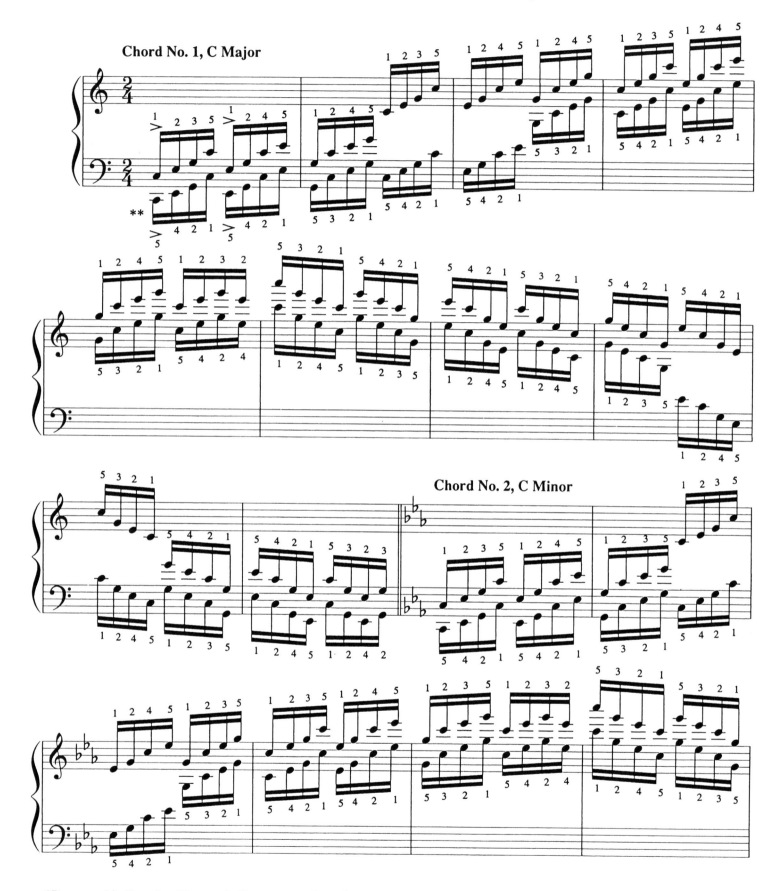

*Presented in Russian Harmonic Pattern; see *Introduction and Guide Book,* Part Three, Chapters VI and VII.
**Accent every downbeat in each group of four notes.

W.M. Co. 11614-E

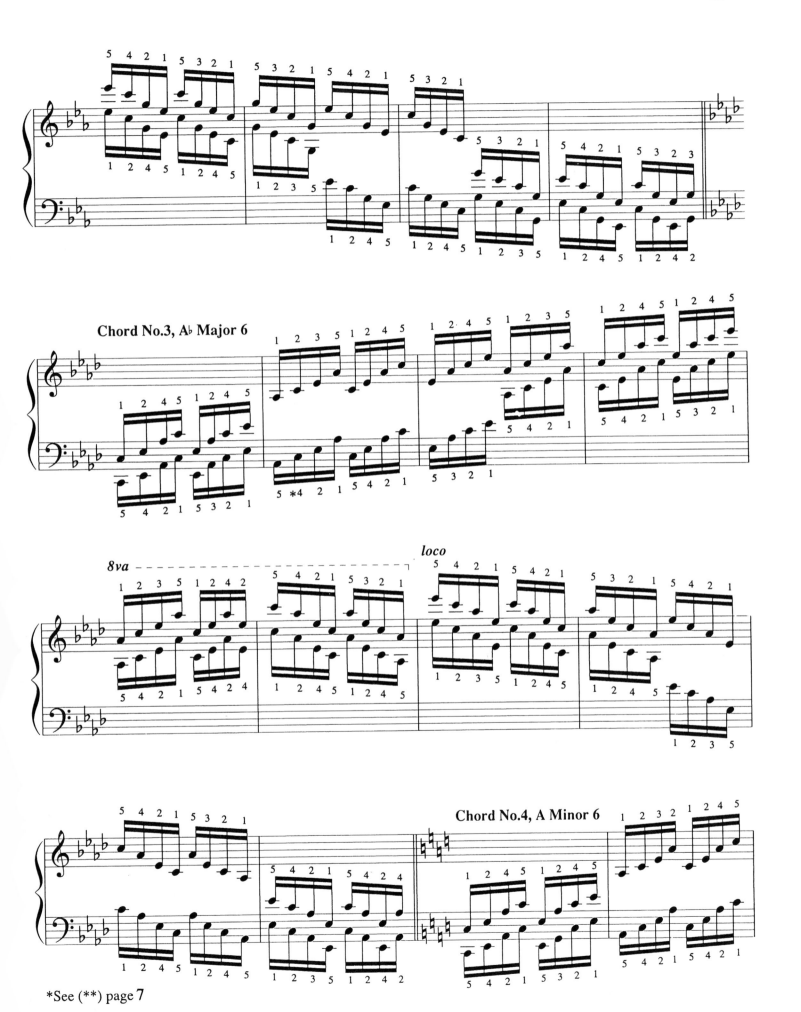

Chord No.3, A♭ Major 6

loco

Chord No.4, A Minor 6

*See (**) page 7

W.M. Co. 11614-E

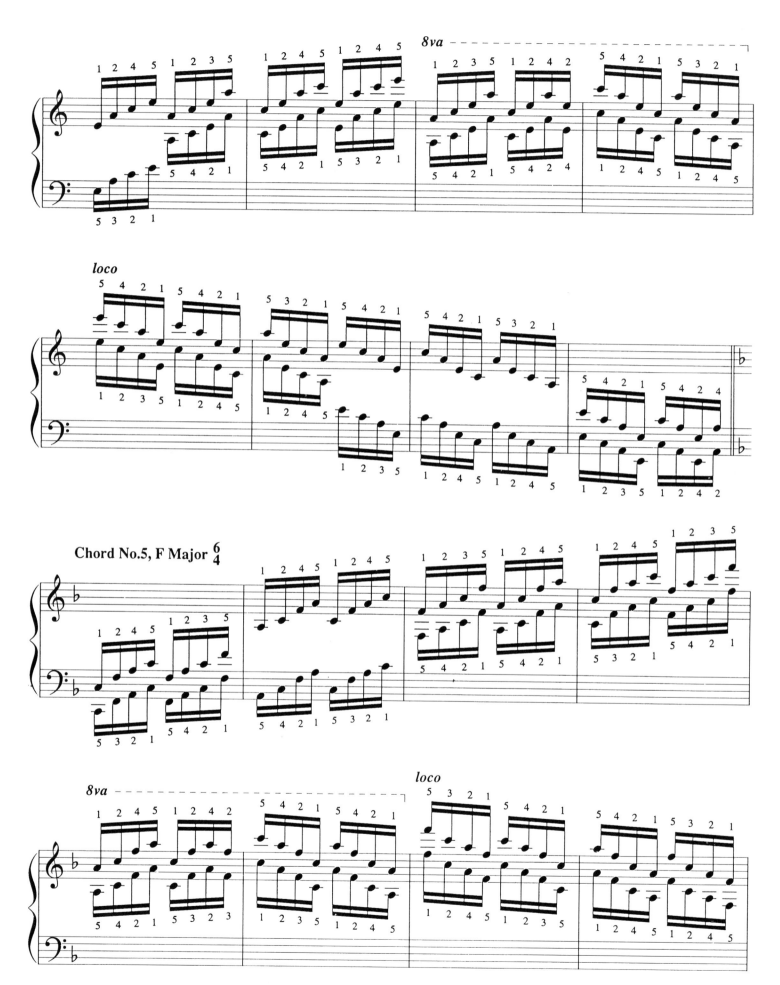

Chord No. 6, F Minor $\frac{6}{4}$

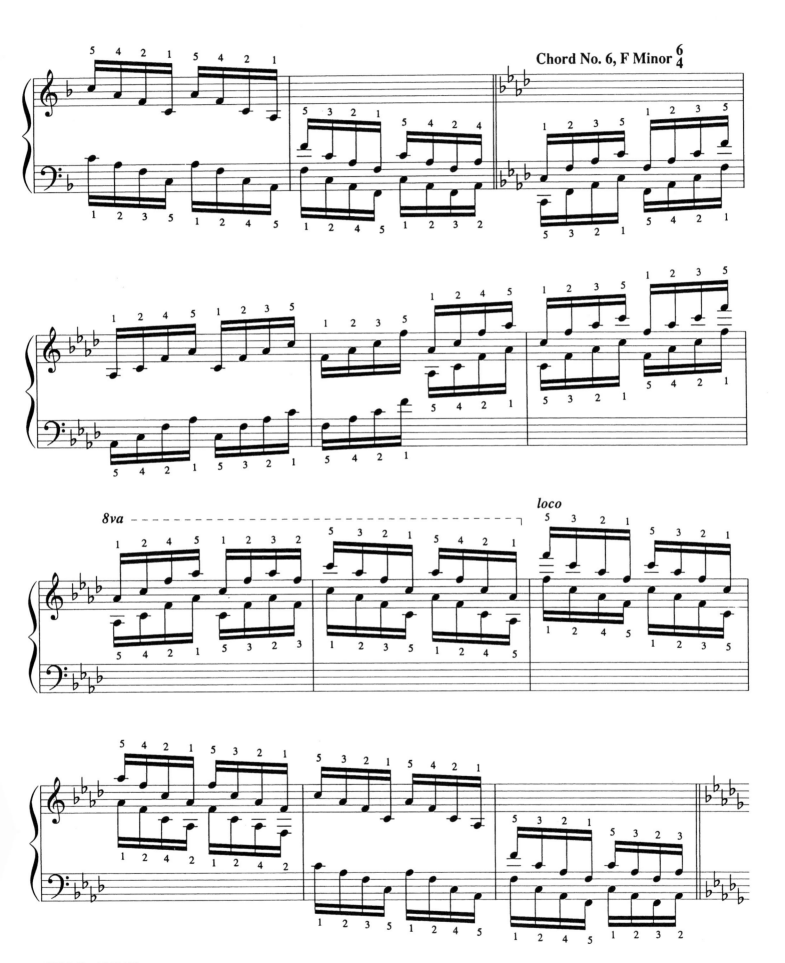

Chord No. 7, vii diminished 7th in D♭ Major

Chord No. 8, V7 in F Major

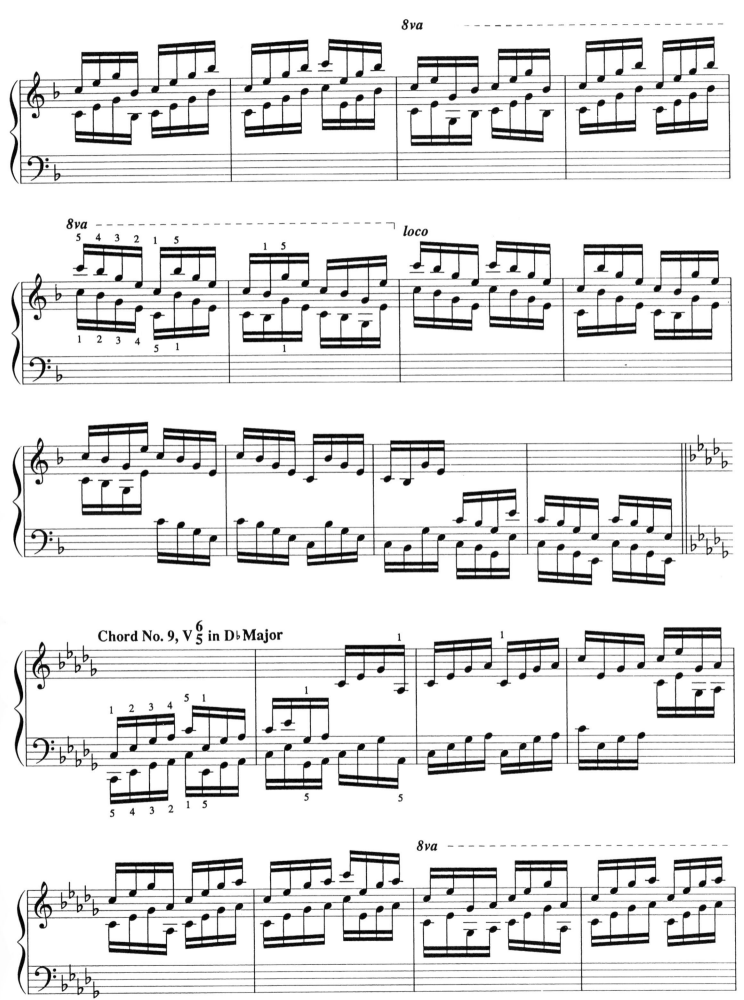

Chord No. 9, V$\frac{6}{5}$ in D♭ Major

Chord No. 10, V $\frac{4}{3}$ in B♭ Major

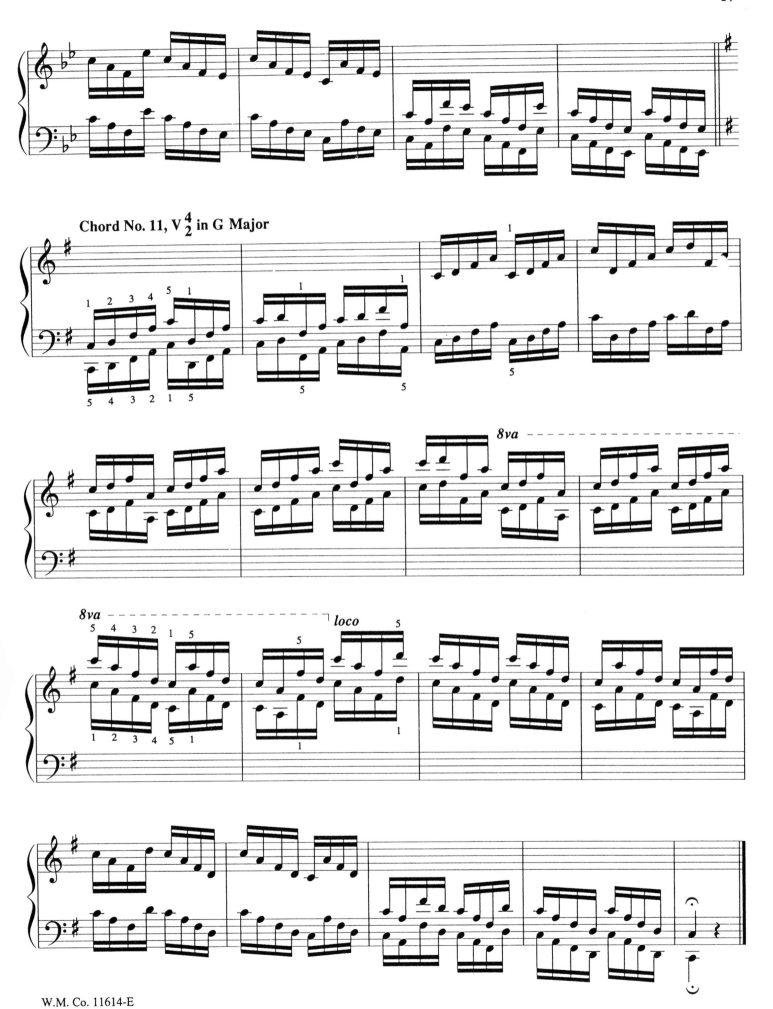

Chord No. 11, V$\frac{4}{2}$ in G Major

Eleven Broken Chords Starting from D♭/C♯

1) D♭ Major

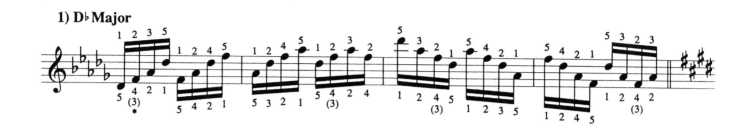

2) C♯ Minor

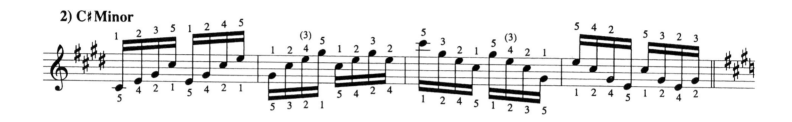

3) A Major 6

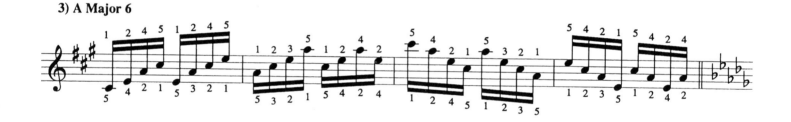

4) B♭ Minor 6

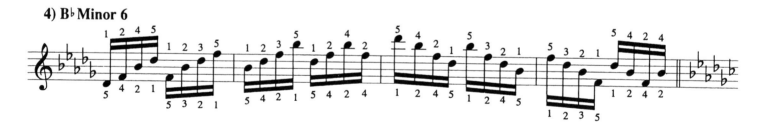

5) G♭ Major $\frac{6}{4}$

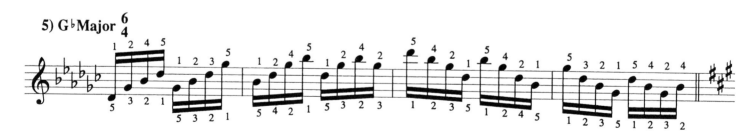

6) F♯ Minor $\frac{6}{4}$

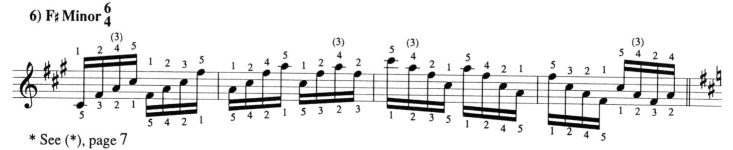

* See (*), page 7

W.M. Co. 11614 - E

7) vii dim. 7th in D Major

8) V7 in D♭ Major

9) V⁶₅ in D Major

10) V⁴₃ in B Major

11) V⁴₂ in A♭ Major

W.M. Co. 11614 - E

Eleven Broken Chords Starting from D

1) D Major

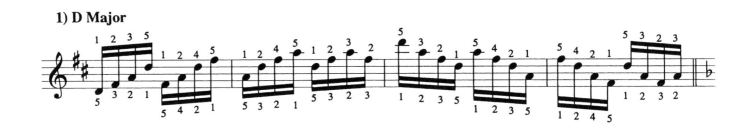

2) D Minor

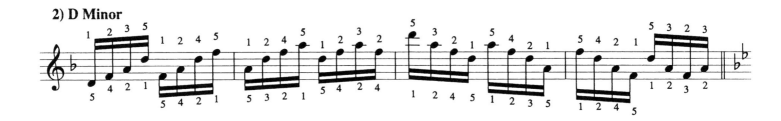

3) B♭ Major 6

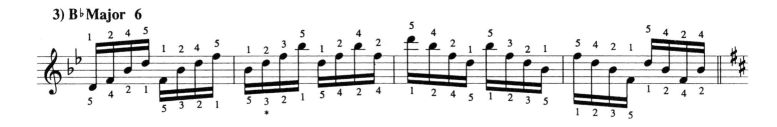

4) B Minor 6

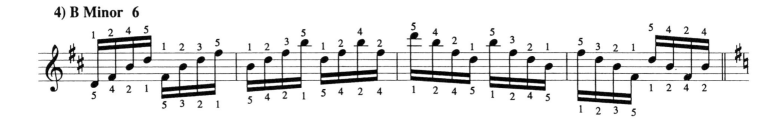

5) G Major $\frac{6}{4}$

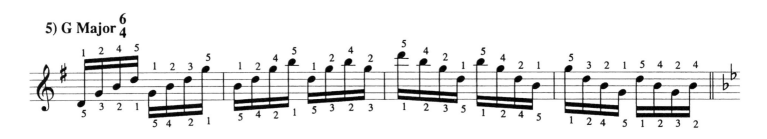

6) G Minor $\frac{6}{4}$

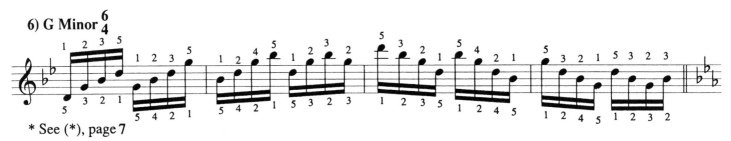

* See (*), page 7

W.M. Co. 11614 - E

7) vii dim 7th in E♭ Major

8) V7 in G Major

9) V$_5^6$ in E♭ Major

10) V$_3^4$ in C Major

11) V$_2^4$ in A Major

Eleven Broken Chords Starting from E♭/D♯

1) E♭ Major

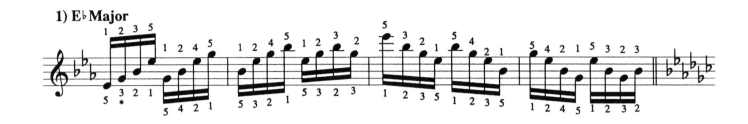

2) E♭ Minor

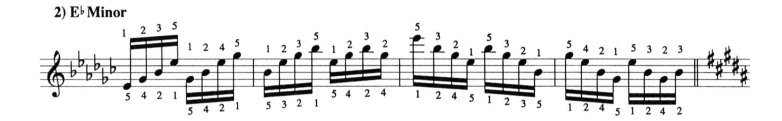

3) B Major 6

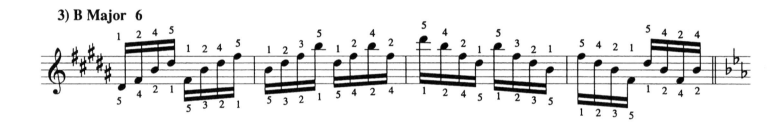

4) C Minor 6

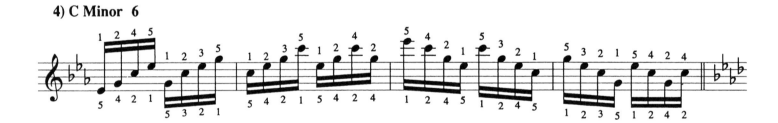

5) A♭ Major $\frac{6}{4}$

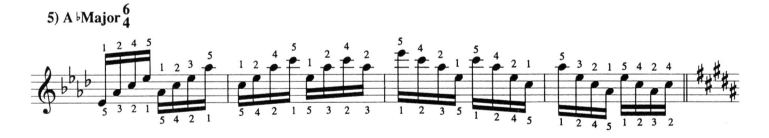

6) G♯ Minor $\frac{6}{4}$

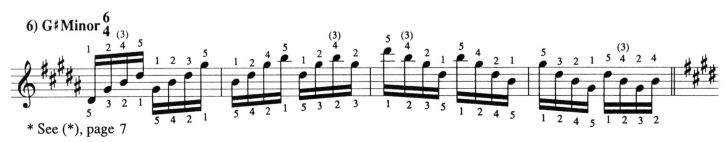

* See (*), page 7

W.M. Co. 11614 - E

7) vii dim. 7th in E Major

8) V7 in A♭ Major

9) V $^6_5$ in E Major

10) V $^4_3$ in D♭ Major

11) V $^4_2$ in B♭ Major

Eleven Broken Chords Starting from E

1) E Major

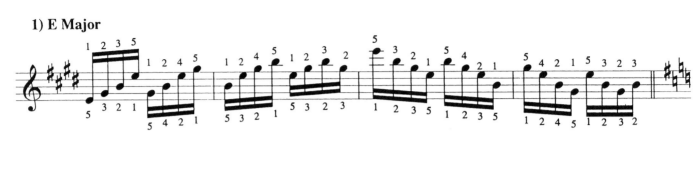

2) E Minor

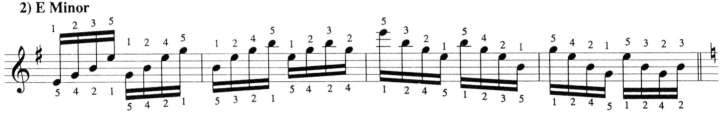

3) C Major 6

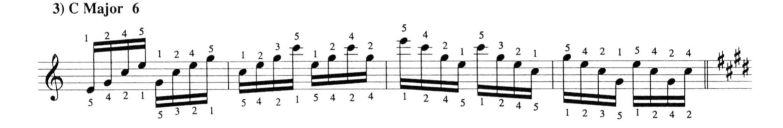

4) C♯ Minor 6

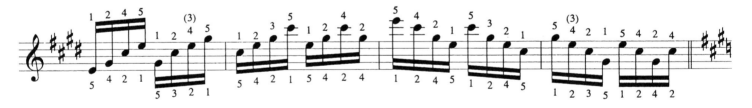

5) A Major 6/4

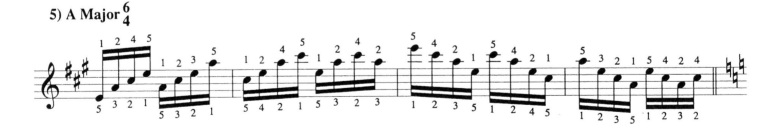

6) A Minor 6/4

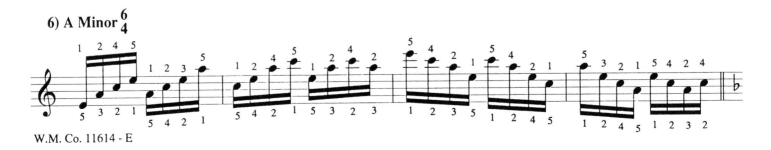

W.M. Co. 11614 - E

7) vii dim. 7th in F Major *

8) V7 in A Major

9) V$_5^6$ in F Major

10) V$_3^4$ in D Major

11) V$_2^4$ in B Major

*The notation of chord No. 7 (diminished 7th) is changed for simpler reading, but the chord remains the same as indicated in the table.

W.M. Co. 11614-E

Eleven Broken Chords Starting from F

1) F Major

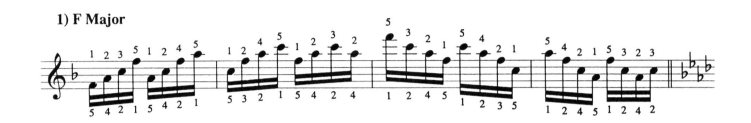

2) F Minor

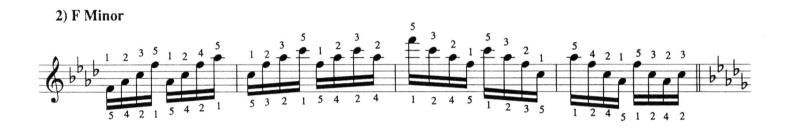

3) D♭ Major 6

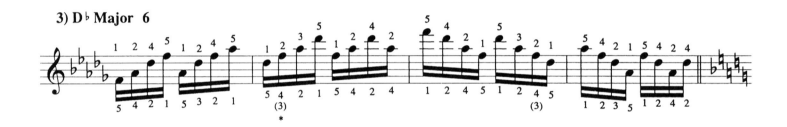

4) D Minor 6

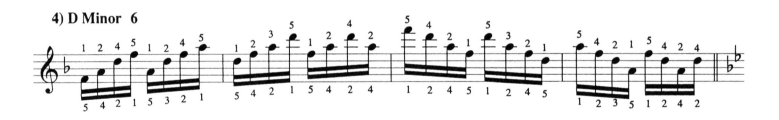

5) B♭ Major ⁶₄

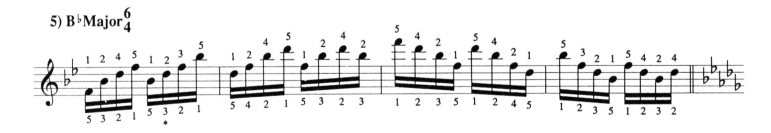

6) B♭ Minor ⁶₄

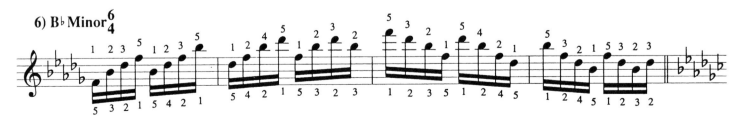

* See (*), page 7.

W.M. Co. 11614 - E

7) vii dim. 7th in G♭ Major *

8) V7 in B♭ Major

9) V 6/5 in G♭ Major

10) V 4/3 in E♭ Major

11) V 4/2 in C Major

*The notation of chord No. 7 (diminished 7th) is changed for simpler reading, but the chord remains the same as indicated in the table.

Eleven Broken Chords Starting from F♯

1) F♯ Major

2) F♯ Minor

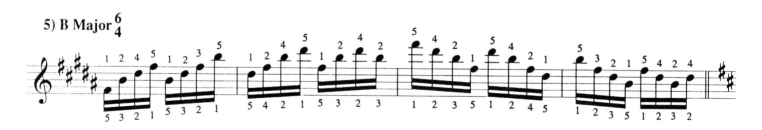

3) D Major 6

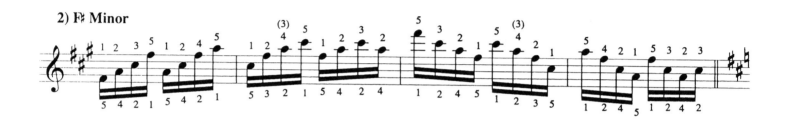

4) D♯ Minor 6

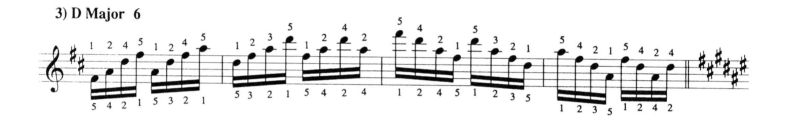

5) B Major 6/4

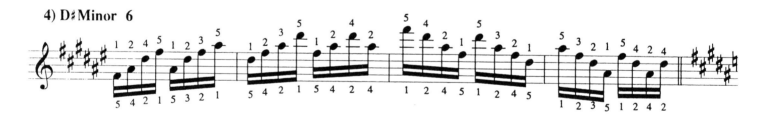

6) B Minor 6/4

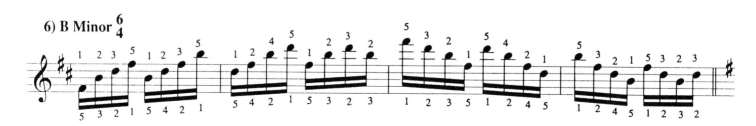

W.M. Co. 11614 - E

7) vii dim. 7th in G Major

8) V7 in B Major

9) V $\frac{6}{5}$ in G Major

10) V $\frac{4}{3}$ in E Major

11) V $\frac{4}{2}$ in C♯ Major

Eleven Broken Chords Starting from G

1) G Major

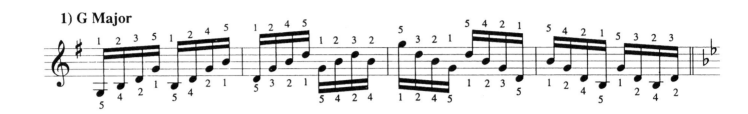

2) G Minor

3) E♭ Major 6

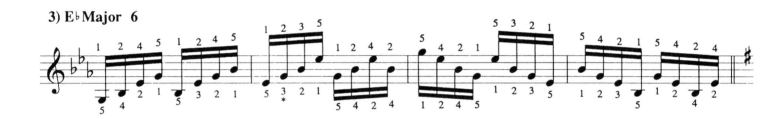

4) E Minor 6

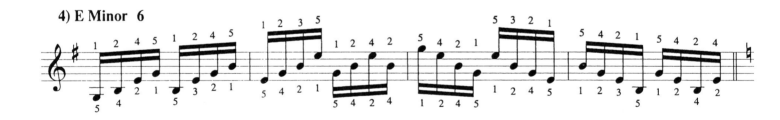

5) C Major 6/4

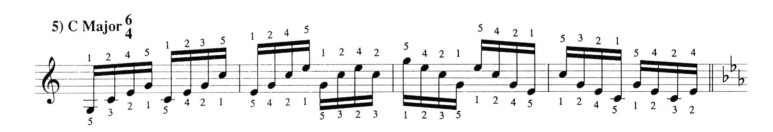

6) C Minor 6/4

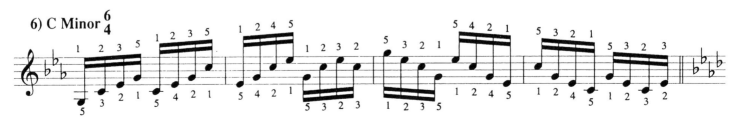

* See (*), page 7.

W.M. Co. 11614 - E

Eleven Broken Chords Starting from A♭ (G♯)

1) A♭ Major

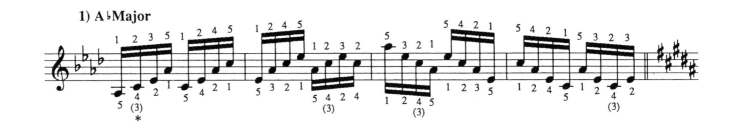

2) G♯ Minor

3) E Major 6

4) F Minor 6

5) D♭ Major 6/4

6) C♯ Minor 6/4

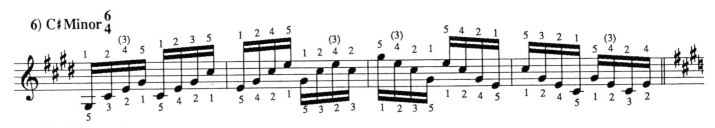

* See (*), page 7.

W.M. Co. 11614 - E

Eleven Broken Chords Starting from A

1) A Major

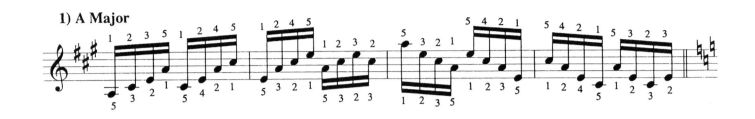

2) A Minor

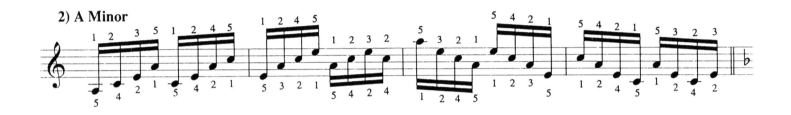

3) F Major 6

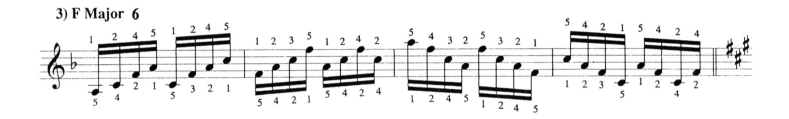

4) F♯ Minor 6

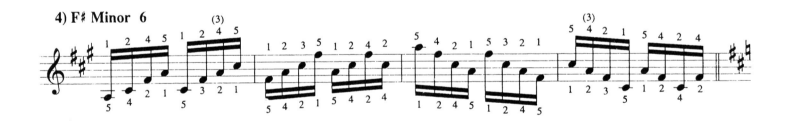

5) D Major 6/4

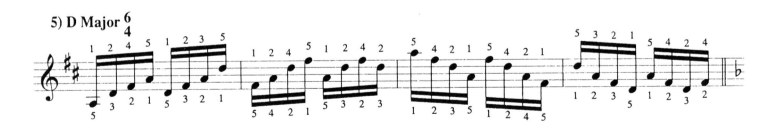

6) D Minor 6/4

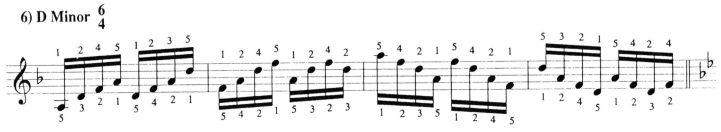

7) vii dim. 7th in B♭ Major

8) V7 in D Major

9) V$^6_5$ in B♭ Major

10) V$^4_3$ in G Major

11) V$^4_2$ in E Major

Eleven Broken Chords Starting from B♭ (A♯)

1) B♭ Major

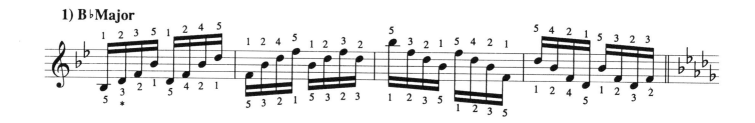

2) B♭ Minor

3) G♭ Major 6

4) G Minor 6

5) E♭ Major $\frac{6}{4}$

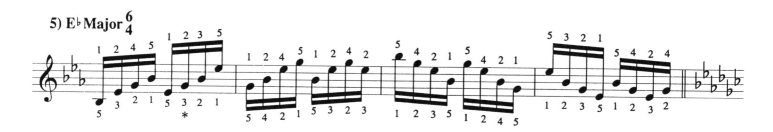

6) E♭ Minor $\frac{6}{4}$

* See (*), page 7.

W.M. Co. 11614 - E

Eleven Broken Chords Starting from B

1) B Major

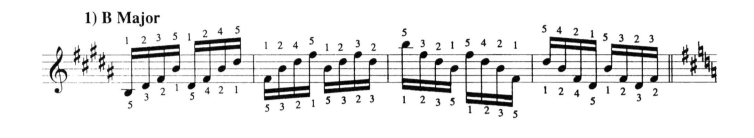

2) B Minor

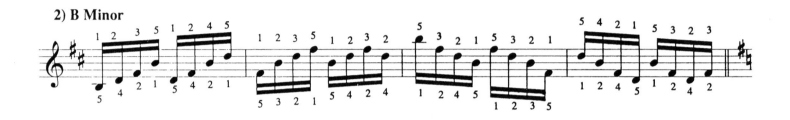

3) G Major 6

4) G♯ Minor 6

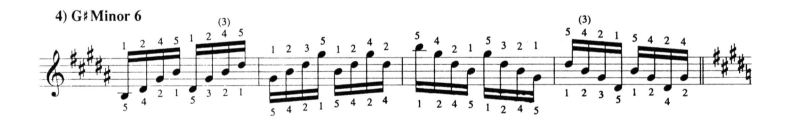

5) E Major $\frac{6}{4}$

6) E Minor $\frac{6}{4}$

Alexander Peskanov
On The Russian Technical Regimen

---Introduction & Guide ("Guide Book").

Complete instructions on how to practice the technical requirements of The Russian Technical Regimen

---Exercise Volume I, Scales in Single Notes

---Exercise Volume II, Broken Chords

---Exercise Volume III, Russian Broken Chords

---Exercise Volume IV, Arpeggios and Block Chords

---Exercise Volume V, Scales in Doubles Notes: thirds, sixths, and octaves

Instructional Videos, "In Search of Sound"

> Demostrations and performances by Alexander Peskanov
>
> (produced by Classical Video Concepts, Inc.)

---Piano Olympics Kit (Manual and Video)

An exciting Piano Event that helps teachers to engage students in practicing scales and exercises using the Russian Technical Regimen. Also, it offers the opportunity to demonstrate their accomplishments in the performance of their repertoire (Produced by Classical Video Concepts, Inc.)

---The Piano Video Exchange with Alek Peskanov

A revolutionary new way of communication between concert artist, student and artist/teacher. This personalized video program will allow the participants to make their own Video Presentation and receive a detailed critique from the artist presented by CVC Inc./Baldwin Piano and Organ Co.

---For further information contact:---
Classical Video Concepts, Inc.
P.O. Box 1930
West Babylon, New York 11704-1930
FAX (516) 669-1203

W.M. Co. 11614E